# HOMOEOPATHIC ARROWS - 3

## CORE & SOUL OF THE REMEDY

DR. SANDEEP SAIRAL

I dedicate this book to all my TEACHERS &

all my PATIENTS who have shown trust on

me.

THANKS.

# Contents

*Foreword* *ix*

*Acknowledgements* *xi*

*Preface* *xiii*

*Prologue* *xv*

1. Aloes 1
2. Arnica Montana 3
3. Arsenic Iodatum 5
4. Aurum Metallicum 7
5. Caladium Seguinum 10
6. Camphora 12
7. Cantharis Vesicatoria 14
8. Carcinosinum 16
9. Chocolate 18
10. Cina Maritima 20
11. Crotalus Horridus 22
12. Cuprum Metallicum 24
13. Elaps Corallinus 26
14. Ferrum Metallicum 28
15. Fluorcum Acidum 31
16. Gelsemium 33
17. Graphites Naturalis 35
18. Ipecacuanha 37
19. Iris-versicolor 39
20. Kalium Bichromicum 41

# Contents

21. Kali-iodatum 43
22. Kreosotum 45
23. Magnesium Carbonicum 47
24. Mezerum 51
25. Natrum Carbonicum 53
26. Podophyllum Peltatum 56
27. Sarasprilla Officinalis 58
28. Sabina 60
29. Selenium 62
30. Tarentula 64
31. Hot & Thirstless 67
**HOT & THIRSTY**
32. Chilly & Thirstless 71
**CHILLY & THIRSTY**
33. Hot Remedies 75
34. Chilly Remedies 76
35. Thirstless Remedies 77
36. Thirsty Remedies 78
37. Warm Foot 79
**WARM SOLE**
38. Cold Foot 83
**COLD SOLE**
39. Warm Hand 87
**WARM PALM**

# Contents

40. Cold Hand 91

**COLD PALM**

41. Miasm-remedies 95

**SYCOSIS-REMEDIES**

**SYPHILIS-REMEDIES**

Conclusion+dream Repertory 101

# Foreword

## HOMOEOPATHIC ARROWS

## 3"D"

<u>*CORE & SOUL OF THE REMEDY*</u>

As this book is focusing on mental generals of **SICK & REMEDY.**

- In mental generals we need to know:-

- Will/ **DESIRES**

- Hates/ **AVERSIONS**

- Loves/ **CRAVING**

- Emotions

- Anger, grief, fear, perversion, sensitivity, greed, **GUILT**, **REGRET**, jealousy, anticipation, suspicion, obstinacy, depression, impulsive, impatience, indifference, speed, reactions (slowness/ hasty), laughing/ weeping, loquacity/ non communicative, consolation.

- Intellect- Memory, concentration, mistakes.

- Understanding- **EASY/ DIFFICULT**, delusion, illusion, hallucination, delirium.

And whatever enter, ***DEEP IN THE MIND.***

***REACHES***the ***SUBCONSCIOUS LEVEL OF MIND***

*Dr. Kent* says – " it is a waste of time to run out all the little symptoms if the remedy has the

**generals.**"

Dr. Kent and his followers says-

" SYMPTOMS OF THE **MIND** ARE THE MOST IMPORTANT SYMPTOMS IN THE REMEDY AND IN THE SICK."

Dr. Kent says " *the **loves and hates or desires*** **and aversions** are the ***deepest*** mental symptoms"

According to my observation and experience I have noticed that **Dreads ,Dreams , and Desires** -(3 "D" ) are all interconnected.

Dreams, Dreads, and Desires **( 3 "D")** Give *insight into the* remedy and sick. While selecting the remedy if we somehow cover these aspects **( 3 "D")** . We can make a *solid and unshakeable prescription.*

**Dr. SANDEEP SAIRAL**

**B.H.M.S.(DELHI).**

# Acknowledgements

***I would like to thanks*** all my patients ,for showing trust on me.

My family for supporting me always.

Thanks .

Dr Sandeep Sairal.

B.H.M.S.(DELHI)

# Preface

**PREFACE**- for **HOMOEOPATHIC ARROWS -(PART-3)**

The intention to write this book is to make homoeopathic prescription more ***sure*** and ***confident***.

*During case taking* we note down the changes in physical and mental generals. We mainly cover (appetite, thirst, temperature, stool , urine, perspiration, sexual drive , fear, behaviour etc).

Actually these all changes are induced by,

***Hypothalamus*** *– pituitary – adrenal axis.*

(as a secondary reaction to illness )

these changes are considered by Homeopathic Physicians as an indication for the selection of their remedy.

{ **HYPOTHALAMUS** =(maintains the ***body's internal balance***, it is body's ***natural homeostatic area)}***

as I mentioned about-

**"HYPOTHALAMUS- PITUITARY- ADRENAL AXIS."**

It justify-

**1}** The **INFINITESIMAL**(SMALL)**DOSE**of homeopathic medicine is enough (just like hormones).

**2}** It also answer how such a infinitesimal (small).

Dose of homoeopathic medicine choose its ***SPHERE OF ACTION***so easily (as hypothalamus govern whole neuro- endocrine) and has its own axis (examples)-

**[ A.**Hypothalamus- Pituitary- Gonadal- Axis**]**

**[ B.**Hypothalamus- Pituitary- Adrenal- Axis**]**

**[** C.Hypothalamus- Pituitary- Thyroid- Axis**]**

**[ D.**Hypothalamus- Posterior- Pituitary**]**

**3}**It also justify when a homoeopath say that **[**x**]**medicine act better in day time or to be **GIVEN IN DAY**

**TIME**and**[Y]**medicine act in different time suppose at night or to be **GIVEN IN NIGHT.**

(As hormones flow or follow ***circadian cycle***).

Above all, I will say never to have **RIGID/FIXED IDEAS** about anything. Always follow & believe in **SCIENTIFIC PROCEDURE OF OBSERVATION**

**DR. SANDEEP SAIRAL**

**B.H.M.S. (DELHI)**

# Prologue

## MATERIA MEDICA

### CONTENT of HOMOEOPATHIC ARROWS- (PART-3):-

1. ALOES
2. ARNICA MONTANA
3. ARSENIC IODATUM
4. AURUM METALLICUM
5. CALADIUM SEGUINUM
6. CAMPHORA
7. CANTHARIS VESICATORIA
8. CARCINOSINUM
9. CHOCOLATE
10. CINA MARITIMA
11. CROTALUS HORRIDUS
12. CUPRUM METALLICUM
13. ELAPS CORALLINUS
14. FERRUM METALLICUM
15. FLUORICUM ACIDUM
16. GELSEMIUM
17. GRAPHITES NATURALIS
18. IPECACUANHA
19. IRIS-VERSICOLOR
20. KALI-BICHROMICUM
21. KALI-IODATUM
22. KREOSOTUM
23. MAGNESIUM CARBONICUM
24. MEZEREUM
25. NATRUM CARBONICUM

26. PODOPHYLLUM PELTATUM
27. SABINA
28. SARASPARILLA OFFICINALIS
29. SELENIUM
30. TARENTULA
31. HOT & THIRSTY/THIRSTLESS
32. CHILLY & THIRSTY/THIRSTLESS
33. HOT REMEDIES
34. CHILLY REMEDIES
35. THIRSTLESS REMEDIES
36. THIRSTY REMEDIES
37. WARM FOOT/SOLE
38. COLD FOOT/SOLE
39. WARM HAND/PALM
40. COLD HAND/PALM
41. MIASM-REMEDIES(PSORA-SYCOSIS-SYPHILIS)

CHAPTER ONE

# ALOES

## ALOES

(HOT & THIRSTY)
LEFT SIDED(1+),
FAST PULSE (1+)

They have **FEAR/DREAD** of **INVOLUNTARY STOOL,** of men, of death, from noise, after pollution, anthrophobia.

They think they will die in a week. So they mingle, socialize, hangout with the whole world. There is pulsation in rectum (due to engorement of veins). There is sense of insecurity in rectum when passing flatus. When passing flatus, there is sensation as if stool would pass with it. **FLATUS IS OFFENSIVE, COPIOUS, BURNING, HOT,***but stool is very little in quantity.*

They have **DREAMS:- STOOL(** means- reflection of freedom),

***soiling themselves with excrement***, becoming- insane, wild, crazy, danger, animals, amorous, and monsters.

< company, **presence of others**, mental exertion, **music,** fasting, fruit, summer season.

They are dissatisfied and angry **about their complaints, on** themselves. Life is a burden for them. Contradiction is intolerant, *they have to restrain themselves to keep away from violence.* They are mischievous, their mood keep on changing, they are vindictive & revengeful. they are hasty in work.

They have **AVERSION** to company after **eating.** They become indolent, or anxious, or they introspect and remain **buried in thought.**

They have **DESIRE** to be silent, of constipation, of urging after eating, urging after passing flatus, of urgring even after stool, sexual **DESIRE** increase after eating or after pollution, cold bathing, **uncovering,** cold air, refreshing things, stimulants, juicy things, apple, salt, tonics.

> **evening,** (irritation, discontent, sadness, indolence)

> **eructation,** passing **flatus**, cold bathing, cold air, long after eating.

CHAPTER TWO

# ARNICA MONTANA

## ARNICA MONTANA-(LEOPARD'S BANE)

(*CHILLY & THIRSTY)*

LEFT SIDED(2+), RIGHT SIDED(2+),
PSORA(1+),
SYCOSIS(1+),
FAST PULSE(3+), SLOW PULSE(1+)

*There are impacts of injuries & troma on both mental & physical generals. They* **DONOT WANTTO BE TOUCHED BOTH MENTALLY & PHYSICALLY.**

They have **FEAR** of being **TOUCHED,** of being struck, by those coming towards them, of crowd, agoraphobia, of others approaching them, of going to doctor, of being injured, of feeling being injured by others, of sudden death when alone at night, of sudden death during heart symptoms, of diseases *(heart disease),* of failure, of something bad will happen, **OF HIGH WALLS & BUILDING WILL FALL UPON HIM,** of incurable disease, of paralysis, misfortune.

They have great **DESIRE** to scratch, just as after injure-**TO SCRATCH THE SCAB OF INJURY.** They scratches lime of the walls. They **DESIRE** to rest, to be silent, uncovering, change of position, open air, impatiently for many thing, cold drinks, pickles, sour, vinegar.

They have **AVERSION** to answer, approach by person, to sympathy, company, thinking, touched, **meat-soup,** sight of food, tobacco smoking *(in accustomed cigar smoker),* to whisky/brandy*(in brandy drinkers).*

< **consolation, talking, thinking***(because they* ***donot want to disturbed/touched mentally),*** shouting, screaming, stretching out affected part, uncovering, walking fast.

> open air, cold bathing, **loosing clothing, letting limbs hang down,** lying on painless side, while fasting, long after eating.

They say they are well, when very sick *(as they* ***do not want to be disturbed both mentally & physically).*** So they want nothing, they are oversensitive to pain. So frightened easily. Nervous cannot bear pain. Whole body over sensitive. Inability to perform, continuous, active work.

They have **DREAM** of **making a long speech** ( means-power of pursuastion),

**being struck by lightining,**

**being buried alive**(means- talent that have not being explored),

funerals, black dog, black cats, physical & mental exertion,

**of muddy water**( means-feeling guilty) ,

graves, exhaustion,

**suffocation**( means- fear & anxiety),

humiliation, shameful, robbers, remorse, quarrels, mutilation, murder, dying, death, **of dead while sleeping on back,** anger, amorous, accidents.

**"NOSE BLEEDING after every fit of COUGHING & after WASHING FACE."**

CHAPTER THREE

# ARSENIC IODATUM

## *ARSENIC IODATUM*

( HOT & THIRSTY) -SENSITIVE TO BOTH HEAT(iod) & COLD(ars).

RIGHT SIDED(1+),

PSORA( 2+),

SYPHILIS(3+),

PULSE FAST( 3+)

**AILMENT from MENTAL WORK.**

They are highly **ANXIOUS, RESTLESS & SAD.** They are sensitive to sensual impression to noise.They are hasty, talkative discontented, irritable & excitable.( anger & irritability during all complaints.)

With dull senses & confusion of mind, they have **DELUSION**" seeing dead person"

They become indifferent to **HAPPINESS, TO LOVED ONES**, to surrounding. ( as they are **DESPAIR & DISCOURAGED)**

They are mild/timid & weep easily.

They have **DREAD/FEAR** of evil, of people( anthropophobia), apprehension, insanity.

They have **AVERSION** to answer, to food, work.

They have **DESIRE** to kill( sudden impulse), uncovering, open air, motion, alcoholic drink.

They have **DREAM of DEAD**, nightmares, vivid, amorous.

< mental exertion, **WARM BED( restlessness), UNDRESSING( skin itching)**, warmth, bathing, washing, physical exertion, **CLOSE ROOM, FAST WALKING,** warm wrap, hunger, apple.

> eating, long after eating, warm wet application.

" losing flesh & weight. **COLDNESS OF HANDS & FOOTS ,FAST PULSE.**"

"There is ***dryness , obstruction , swelling ( inside nose).* Smell lost. nasal discharge( like honey) + constant desire to sneeze".**

CHAPTER FOUR

# AURUM METALLICUM

## AURUM METALLICUM-METALLIC GOLD

*(CHILLY & THIRSTY)*

RIGHT SIDED(3+),
PSORA(1+),
SYCOSIS(1+),
SYPHILIS(3+),
FAST PULSE(3+)

For clearly visible "**DEPRESSED PATIENTS.**"

They sit as if wrapped in deep sad thought completely reserved nature. One of my patient, when he first time come with his son to my clinic, sits silently & said nothing *(depressed)* trying to hide true feelings. They seem to have secretive & quiet disposition.

They seem to be joyless, having lack of initiative for anything. there is **loss of will** from melancholia. They **feels unfortunate.** In whole case taking they will never smiles. They lack self esteem. They feel they will never succeed. **They feel sorry for themselves.** They become pessimist. They feel they cannot do things fast enough. They grief about their condition. Discouraged, discontented with themselves. Disgust with everything. Doubtful/ despair about recovery, despair with pains, about themselves & others .

There is self **roasting/disapproval/criticism.** This lack of self confidence, make them unhappy with themselves. They feel or have convict of neglecting something, their duty or friends.

They have delusion of they do everything wrong, they cannot succeed, unfit for world, friends have lost confidence in them. They are **completely demoralized.** For any situation in life **resignation, surrender or quiting** is easy option for them.

They have **FEAR** of **neglecting their duty,** robbers, **crowd, of people,** anthropophobia, of suicide, **death,** heart disease, high places.

They have **DREAM** of **darkness,**

falling from height or high place( means- feeling out of control),

robbers ( means-feeling insecure & weak),

**mentalexertion,** exhausting, frightful, quarrels, violence, **death,** dead bodies, amorous, anger.

They have **DESIRE** of DEATH(one of my patient revealed this desire as she lost her husband due to covid & was left with child with special need), hide, **hasty to do several things at once,** travel, to be killed, **solitude, to besilent, diverted from thought of themselves,** cold drink, coffee.

> Occupied/diverted, music, after eating, flatus, walking slowly, summer, cold bathing.

< Presence of others, company, consolation, conversation, mental exertion, talk of others, thinking of complaints, contradiction is intolerable, uncovering, walking fast, **sensitive to smell of sweet.**

They have **AVERSION** to answer, **company, presence of others,** approach by person, to family members, to all person, **mental work,** uncovering, **going out,** food, meat.

" Sadness **in amenorrhoea."**

" Praying aloud in sadness"

" **They do rapid questioning without waiting for a reply."**

" There is profound despondency with **increased blood pressure."**

" **Erethism or vascular fullness** characterizes nearby all complaints."

CHAPTER FIVE

# CALADIUM SEGUINUM

## CALADIUM SEGUINUM-(AMERICAN ARUM)

*(HOT & THIRSTLESS)*

SYCOSIS(1+),

FAST PULSE(2+)

Absent mindedness/forgetfulness in persons ***who are mentally & physically prostrated from sexual excess & tabacco smoking.*** You cannot cure these patients, if they do not have DESIRE for improvement/ redesigning/ renovation/ correction. patients must use their will power to help the remedy & themselves.

There is prostration of mind from mental exhaustion, leads to weakness of memory- for what they had just done or for occurrence of the day.

this forgetfulness is especially from tabacco smoking or after sexual excess. there lascivious fancies with impotency. They have sexual desire with no ability or automatic erection without desire, sometimes no erection even after caress in males, coition enjoyment is absent. There is irritability after coition. There is ***itching in the***

***scrotum at night & perspiration in the scrotum also.*** There is sadness from masturbation/ pollution/ with impotency.

In female there is want of orgasm. There is **voluptuous itching in vagina & withitching sexual desire increased** leading to nymphomania *(disposition to masturbation).* They feels restlessness **after smoking** or during headache.

They are sensitive to noise, they get easily started especially from *(when a door slams),* they get frightened easily even from their own shadow. They weep like a child about illness with senseless chatter. They keep on talking *(excessive),* they are hasty while eating. They get discomfort after pickled fish.

**"THEY HAVE ANXIETY WHILE SHAVING"**

**DREAM** - recalling thing long forgotten, murder, of people not seen for years, fight, of long past event, of dead, amorous.

**FEAR** - **of his own shadow,** to go to sleep, of motion, from noise, of misfortune, **of being injured,** of **infection,** of exertion, of evil, of impending disease, of death, if dark, **of cutting himself when shaving.**

**DESIRE** - to drink with thirstlessness, **for defecation while smoking,** uncovering, hot & warm drinks, tabacco smoking, sexual desire increased with itching in females.

**AVERSION** - cold drinks, cold water, milk, motion.

< mental exertion, of clothing, **scratching,*chocolate*,** deep breathing, fish, dry food, sour, vinegar, lying in bed, pressure, **rubbing,** sitting erect, **before sleep, at beginning of sleep, during sleep,** tabacco, **whenbreaking off tabcco smoking, touch,** walking, **warmth of bed.**

> **suppression of sexual desire,** perspiration, after sleep, waking, getting feet wet.

CHAPTER SIX

# CAMPHORA

## CAMPHORA

*(CHILLY + THIRSTY/ THIRSTLESS)*

PSORA(1+),

FAST PULSE(2+), SLOW PULSE(2+)

In acute complaints there is violent **thirst** in chronic complaints **thirstless.**

It antidotes most of the medicines *(sudden onset)* sudden sinking of strength.

There is delusion of being **alone in the world.**

There is feeling of being **dumped, neglected/ abandoned.** There is sensation of isolation. There is timidity especially when going to bed. They get tortured by religious ideas mostly at night. They make wild gestures,***(wild dancing)*** *with rage, they swallows their own feces. They do biting, spitting, tearing clothes & everything,* (destructiveness regarding clothes), they **strike their chest themselves.** They weep after anxiety or sometimes causeless, discouraged.

Their speech, movement & occupation **speed are hasty.** Their understanding is easy but they have difficulty in concentration.

There is icy coldness of whole body, cold perspiration, yet they have **AVERSION to covers.** But they are excessivly sensitive to cold air. Nothing satisfies them. They become shamless, nymphomanic, obsence. They wants to be naked or **bares breast.** They want to **lie on bare floor.** There is sensation of flying. They have disposition to contradict with repulsive mood. They get offended easily takes everything in bad part.

**<when alone, covers(so they kick them off), warm wrap,** darkness, shining objects.

> diverted/ occupied, **uncovering/ undressing/** discharges, mucus secretion, perspiration, **thinkingof complaints,** drinking cold water, pressure, rubbing.

**AVERSION - solitude,** cover *(intolerance), being touched, potatoes, to bed.*

**DESIRE - company,** diverted from thought of themselves to weep all time but eyes are dry, uncovering, cold air, must have windows open, to hide, to kill, to bite.

They have **FEAR of their own thought, to go to sleep,** of being drawn upward, of people *(anthropophobia),* of mirrors in room, **of death, of impending danger, of being alone at night,** of open window/ knife. Due to **FEAR** they walk until they have perspiration *(which make them better).*

They have **DREAMS** of **death, dying, frightful,** ghosts, **nightmares, amorous,** being busy, business, excelling in mental work, mental exertion, previous events.

**" profuse sweating only on uncovered parts "**

CHAPTER SEVEN

# CANTHARIS VESICATORIA

## CANTHARIS VESICATORIA-(SPANISH FLY)

*(CHILLY & THIRSTY)*

RIGHT SIDED(3+),LEFT SIDED(1+),
PSORA(1+),
SYCOSIS(1+),
SLOW PULSE(1+), FAST PULSE(1+)

**Sudden** onset. Its action is **rapid** & **intense.** The local inflammatory condition come on with **great rapidity** & this brings the patient down violently sick in a **great hurry, restlessness** drive them from place to place roving about aimlessly. They must have constantly. They undertakes many thing, but perserves in nothing ending in **RAGE.** In **rage** they tear their own hair, tear themselves to pieces with nails.

Disposition to **be angry** & to fly into rage. Disposition to contradiction. Actually their strength increases with this insanity. They keep themselves fruitlessly busy, **walk hastly.**

They become **irritable during pain** & from insult.

They have **DELUSION** of **someone is under bed,** of someone bouncing them **up & dowd in bed,** of **choked by icy - cold hands,** of hearing foot steps, of hearing knocking under **bed,** of someone with ice - cold hands took them by the throat. They get frighten easily.

They have **FEAR** of **bed,** of death, **of eating,** after eating food, of water, of **mirrors** in room. They have **FEAR** with anxiety.

They have **AVERSION** to being touched, **food,** approach by person, bathing, drinking cold water.

< uncovering, washing, bathing, cold air, conversation, talking, touch, **shinning objects,** seeing or hearing running **water,** drinking coffee.

They **DESIRE** to be silent, to bite, meat.

> walking fast, perspiration, hot foot, warm air.

They have **DREAM** of **forest** ***(mean you need to slow down).***

**DREAM** of **STAG** *(means you take* ***hasty decision****).*

**DREAM** of **COOKING** *(means* ***you care more about your loved,*** *than yourself).*

**DREAM** of quarrel *(means dissatisfaction with your person life).*

**DREAM** of walking in woods *(means you are moody & donot like to* ***reveal everything****)*

**DREAM** of falling *(means hidden* ***insecurities,*** *social* ***anxieties,*** *or unstable situation in life).*

Other **DREAM** are of being busy, people, companies, nightmares & amorous.

**" intolerate, constant urging, painful, burning urination as a concomitant in any diseased condition".**

CHAPTER EIGHT

# CARCINOSINUM

## *CARCINOSINUM*

Affected by extreme of climates.

Ailments from-Humilaion, grief, excitement,***anticipation***, reproach, ***rudeness of others***, work.

They are yielding & **timid** personality. They **weep** after anxiety ,from reproaches, from sympathy with others, when criticised, when reprimanded, scolded, music, sometimes even causeless. As they are sensitive to sensual impression, rudeness, reproaches, criticism, pain, noise, music.

They *love animals*, to watch thunderstorm( as they are over sensitive to enviorment)

They are dissatisfied with surrounding.They ***worry*** about their **WORK & BUSINESS.** They are passionate, industrious, workalcoholic, fastidious, impatience, anxious & restless.

They constantly dwell on their condition. (As they are sad about their health). They are despair of recovery .They keep***bitting their nail.*** They feel unfortunate. They have undemonstrative/reserved/remote/grief. They donot cry after grief.( Hide true feeling).

They are impelled to touch everything. They have monomania, mania of cleanness & washing. (They **always washes their hand)**

They have **DELUSION** as if been poisoned or their arms donot belong to them.

They have **FEAR/DREAD** of being **LATE**.( They ***always hurry to arrive for appointed time***),

They **FEAR** about ***health of loved persons***, of pain, incurable(disease), death, busy street, in a crowd, of animals, of dark, ***dogs,*** of failure, **BEFOREEXAMINATION**, of suicide, of snake, of strangers, of not being able to bear any medicine, of water, of thunderstorm.

They **DESIRE** to ***travel,*** wander, ***to bite fingers***, death, to be silent, mental work, ***chocolate, eggs,*** milk, ***salt,*** spices.

They have **AVERSION** to all person, solitude, conversation, music, eggs, fruit, ***milk, salt.***

**<*reprimand*,** conversation, consolation, alone, thunderstorm, sea shore air, bathing in sea, undressing.

> consolation( kind words), dancing, music, ***occupied/ diverted***, thunderstorm, sea shore air, storm weather, ***short sleep***, lying knee elbow position.

Children are oversensitive, wild, restless & sometimes dul & ill humoured **(*get easily offended*)**

There can be **FAMILY HISTORY** /blood relation of carcinoma, T.B. ,anaemia, D.M. & suicide.

CHAPTER NINE

# CHOCOLATE

**CHOCOLATE-(** Theobronea Caco)

(THIRSTY & CHILLY)

They become irritable when disturbed, from little things, when aroused, before menses, especially toward **CHILDREN**( They attempts to escape from their family & children). As they **wish/want** to be alone/quiet. They have anxiety from anticipation & about **MONEY MATTER**.

They have difficulty while driving/reading & studying. As they keep wandering ,mostly disconnected( Due to **INTERNAL RESTLESSNESS**).

They laugh easily, become happy with ***bird sound/ song***(music). Feeling relaxed.

They have **DELUSION** that they are **ANIMAL**, of back open & forming **WINGS, BLOOD** pouring out of mouth, **HAIRY** animal(baby), people are RAT & mice, world is on fire, they are **BEING WATCHED**, hair are cut short & bristly.

They have **FEAR/DREAD** of **ANIMALS**, of being **BITTEN**, of **DOGS**, of impending danger, high walls building fall upon him, of falling , something bad will happen, **BEING OBSERVED**, men, of their condition, BEING INJURED.

They have AVERSION to **CHILDREN, HUSBAND, CONVERSATION, COMPANY,** colour( blue, green , maroon), cooked food, fat & rich food, solid food, **ICE-CREAM, TEA**, sweeet.

They have **DESIRE** to bite, wear colour(yellow , brown), hide, **LAUGH, WANDER, TRAVEL**, COVER, **CHOCOLATE,** fizzy drinks, cold drinks, juicy fruits, ICE, ORANGES, **BLACK PEPPER, RED PEPPER**, red food, sausages, FLY, stroke her hair.

< **COMPANY, CHOCOALTE,** sweet, TEA, warm drinks, artificial light.

> ALONE, during eating, COVER, lying knee-chest position, warm wrap.

They have **DREAMS** of **being ACCUSED OF THEFT(** means- feeling of guilt),

unsuccessful efforts, people(crowd),

**journey by car**( means- life is moving/happening not dull or stagnant),

injury, hurried,

**GYPSIES ( m**eans misguided expectation or desire to roam without responsibility & obligation), **GUNS**( i had one teenage girl patient with this dream), fruits, friends, **MARKETS( means**- unexpected upcoming adventures),

hung with married men in **FALLING LIFT shat ( means**- crisis situation) , friend FALLING from a window, **of losingtheir own FAMILY**, own family,

of **FORTUNE TELLERS** (means- lack of confidence or you are not sure about the decision you are making),

growing things,

**being PREGNANT**( means- new begining or something life changing).

" **POSITIVENESS, CREATIVE, SELFISH**"

CHAPTER TEN

# CINA MARITIMA

## *CINA- ( Worm seed)*

(HOT & THIRSTY)

**LEFT SIDED** (3+),

**PULSE FAST**(2+),

PSORA(1+)

**AILMENTS** from -**FRIGHT** , vexation, ***anger***, **WORMS.**

Due to **WORM AFFECTION**, there will be irritabilty, rage. There is **WILDNESS, RUDENESS, NAUGHTINESS** in children. They **WEEP** when ***touched,*** on waking, during stool, after coughing, **WHENTHEIR WILL ARE NOT DONE**, from ***caressing***. They **become STIFF & KICK when CARRIED**. Costantly digging & boring at the NOSE. ( Itching of NOSE), Grinding teeth during sleep.They are quarrelsome & obstinate.

They have **AVERSION** to **BEING CARESSED**, approach by person, to play( in children), ***being touched,*** milk, mother's milk, motion.

They have **DESIRE** to bite, ***to be carried***( especially over shoulder), to pull one's hair, to be silent, full of desire( numerous),cold food, cold drink, sweet , bread.

They have **FEAR/DREAD** of **TOUCH**(cannot bear to have anyone come near them especially in children), evil.

They have **DREAM** of striving, NIGHTMARES, absurd, exhaustion, business of the day.

> ROCKING FAST, continued motion, **lying on ABDOMEN**, darkness, milk, walking.

< MENTAL EXERTION, reading, presence of STRANGERS, fast walking, **TOUCH,** ***during & after sleep***, ***hunger***, fasting, mother's milk, sweet, **pepper.**

CHAPTER ELEVEN

# CROTALUS HORRIDUS

## CROTALUS HORRIDUS-(POISON OF RATTLE SNAKE)

*(HOT & THIRSTY)*

RIGHT SIDED (3+),

SYCOSIS(1+),

SYPHILIS(1+),

SLOW PULSE(2+)

PAIN APPEAR SUDDENLY(2+)

In one of my case of **bladder & postrate cancer,** with blood in urine, due to painful retension of urine, He was on **urinary catheter.** I used this remedy as intercurrent remedy.

**Tissue rapidly** decompose, produce putrid & malignant condition.

They have **antipathy to their family.** They have delusion as if **surrounded by enemies** or pursued by enemies, or they are in **journey** restlessness drive them from **place to place.** They attempts to escape. They are **intolerant of pressure & clothing.** They have weakness of memory for expressing themselves. Although they are loquacious, vivacious& timid with thought of death. They are forgetful of well known street.

They have **FEARof serious thoughts, of walking across busy street**, of people, **crowd,** public places, of not able to bear any medicine.

They have **AVERSION to family members,** to all person, solitude, **meat.**

< **clothing,** touch, spring, summer.

> drinking, **fanned,** walking.

They have **DESIRE** for company ,sweet.

They have **DREAM of** travelling/ journey( means- movement in life),

quarrels, anger,

**drowning of dead bodies**( means- emotional rebirth),

smell of dead bodies, dead bodies, churchyard,

***of being in graveyard( means-*** *fear of new/ future, or lack of confidence).*

" **decrease clotting** / coagulation in **blood.**"

CHAPTER TWELVE

# CUPRUM METALLICUM

## CUPRUM METALLICUM

*(THIRSTY)*

PSORA(2+),

PULSE SLOW(2+), FAST SLOW(1+)

They have **FEAR** of people (*anthropophobia),* strangers, of **others** approaching them, they **cannot bear to have anyone** come near them, *(so they have* ***desire*** *to escape).* They have **FEAR** of misfortune, of death, of dark, of accident, of water, of **downward motion,** of falling.

They have **AVERSION** to company, **presence of others** *(so they avoids the* ***sight of people),*** to answer, being touched, to bed, to everything, cooked food.

< **company, darkness,** mental exertion, touch, walking fast, ***beans, peas***, cabbage, flatulent food, heavy food, hot drink, hot food, milk, meat, sauerkraut, indigestible.

> occupied/ diverted, perspiration, cold bathing, mucus secretion, discharge, long after eating, cold food, cold drinks, letting limbs hangs down.

They **DESIRE** to bite, to kill, to escape, to hide, to go home, solitude, to be silent, to play *(night),* to pull ones hair, to be magnetized, sour, from prostration of mind, mental exhaustion there is **slowness in mind,** they became irresolute, they have timidity to talk in public, they get frightened easily sluggish, dull, discouraged. Development of children get arrested. They **passes feces on the floor.**

They have delusion as if **selling vegetables,** pursued by enemies, police. Delusion that they are officer, or a commander/ general. Delusion that they are **repairing old chairs** or about to be arrested.

They are vindictive, impulsive & **hasty while eating.** They talk with air of command ***(dictatorial).***They have disposition to contradict. There are attacks of unconquerable anxiety restlessness drive them from place to place.

" **cough > by drinking cold water.**"

"**spasms, cramps or convulsive** tendency associated itself **with almost every complaints.**"

CHAPTER THIRTEEN

# ELAPS CORALLINUS

## *ELAPS-(Coral Snake)*

(THIRSTY & CHILLY)

**RIGHT** SIDED

**AILMENTS** from **ANTICIPATION.**

They have **FEAR/DREAD-*something bad will happen, of death***, of apoplexy, of being alone( solitude), ***snake***, **RAIN**, robbers, impending disease.

They become **SAD** during **WET WEATHER**, especially anxiety ( due to **RAIN**). They feel ,they must shout/ scream.They sit still, buried in thoughts, They become forgetful due to mental exhaution. Concentration become difficult, due to prostration of mind.

They have **DELUSION** of ***hearing,*** *being injured, being beaten , falling forward.*

They have **DREAMS** of weeping, business,

**FALLING INTO A PIT/ABYSS** ( ***bottomless pit)( means***- restriction & obstacle in life).,

***dead bodies,*** nightmares, remorse, of dead, falling.

They have **DESIRE** to bite themself, ***company( as if something horrible may happen if alone***), to **PLAY INGRASS**, **TRAVEL**, open air, striking, to be in

***cavern(cave)***, to be silent(during menses), **ICE**, oranges, **SALAD**, sour, **MILK**, buttermilk, SWEETS.

They have **AVERSION** to **BANANAS**, meat, oranges, plums, sour, cold drink, water, bread, to speak.

< presence of others, talks of others, while alone, **CLOTHING(** ***near external throat)***, cold bathing, cold air, during **RAIN/WET WEATHER**, fruit.

> **lying on ABDOMEN** , night seminal emission.

"Desquamation of **FINGER TIPS, BLACK EAR WAX** ".

"Non coaguable hemophilia, **BLACK DISCHARGE, DARK CLOTS**".

CHAPTER FOURTEEN

# FERRUM METALLICUM

## *FERRUM METALLICUM*

(CHILLY & THIRSTLESS)

LEFT SIDED( 2+)

PULSE FAST (2+)

PSORA(1+)

SYCOSIS(2+)

**AILMENTS** from - being scorned, excitement, silent grief.

They are egoistic, selfcontented with haughty look. Their mood keep on alternating( weeping & laughing at climacteric). They become ill humour **duringFEVER OR DURING & AFTER MENSES.** There is sadness, calmness & soberness. But little things seem important. They are sensitive to noise. They become **IRRITABLE** from noise, **during HEAT, or DURING & AFTER MENSES.**

They have disposition to contradict, But for themself **CONTRADICTION** is intolerable.( They become violent & easily anger from contradiction). They seems to be hysterical & hypochondriac. They get **EXCITED** over little things. **(from-slightest CONTRADICTION, during HEAT, or DURING & AFTERMENSES.**

They are dictatorial, dissatisfied & restless.

They have **DELUSION** of **BEING at WAR**, of water, in dark, people walking behind.

Menses are either amenorrhoea, or copious, frequent, prolonged, metrorragia. **ANAEMIA, FAINTNESS, WEAKNESS after HAEMORRHAGE.** Although they will look strong( PSEUDO-PLETHORA). So, **COLDNESS OF HANDS & FOOT.** ***Cold, profuse, clampy perspiration.***

They have **DREAD/FEAR of GOING BY RAIL,** of misfotune, of death,of people/crowd/public place, crossing bridge, noise, apprehension with anxiety. fear with palpitation.

They have **AVERSION** to friends, company( avoid sight of people), conversation, thinking, mental work, noise, hot food, hot drink,fat, rich food, meat, egg, milk, **SOLID FOOD.**

They have **DESIRE** -to be silent, to walk, to weep, uncover, bread, butter, hot food, **LIQUID FOOD**, meat, **RAW TOMATATOES,** wam drink, warm food, warm soup, sour, sweets, indigestible things( lime , slate, chalk).

They have **DREAM** of water, battles, amorous, dead, dead relatives,

**DEAD FRIENDS(** means- you wish your friend were around you to help/navigate you),

fights,

falling into water( means- suppressed feeling or emotions),

nightmare, intellectual,

seeing again an **OLD SCHOOLMATE**( means- nostalgic mood),

long past events, death of long **deceased FRIENDS.**

< sympathy(anger), presence of other, company( even of **INTIMATE FRENDS)**, **CONTRADICTION,** talks of others, **TALKING,** conversation, **EXCITMENT**, after slight haemorrhage, touching hair, perspiration, cold open air, **cover(INTOLERANCE), while FASTING, DRY FOOD, EGGS**, fat, fruit, meat, hot drink, hot food, rich food, sweets, **TEA**, after long sleep, tobacco, warm wrap, **FAST WALKING.**

> **ALONE**, motion( **CONFUSION)**, mental exertion, **OCCUPIED & DIVERTED, exertion ( SADNESS)**, uncovering, **EATING(perspiration)**, carrying, long after eating, **BEING FANNED, WALKING SLOWLY**, after sleep, cold food, milk, tea, haemorrhage, dry/windy weather.

CHAPTER FIFTEEN

# FLUORCUM ACIDUM

## *FLUORICUM ACIDUM*

( HOT & THIRSTY)

FAST PULSE( 1+)

PSORA(1+)

SYCOSIS( 2+)

SYPHILIS(2+)

**AILMENTS** from- **ANTICIPATION,** erruption of **WISDOM TEETH**, mental work.

It is one of deepest & slowest remedy. ***With strangers they are cheerful/lively/optimist***. But indifference to **BUSINESS, FAMILY, PARENTS , WIFE** & loved ones. They have indiffernce to important things( As they ***donot realise their responsiblities***). They have laschivious, **LUSTFUL**, & sexual behaviour( **SATYRIASIS, NYMPHOMANIA**).

They have **DELUSION** -To **must DISSOLVE MARRIAGE**, They **must DRIVE CHILDREN OUT of theHOUSE**, They ***must get rid of servants***.

They have **AVERSION** to **FAMILY MEMBERS, PARENTS,** friends, **WIFE, BUSINESS**, sour, coffee.

They have **DESIRE** to **LEAVE HOME**, to walk, **WASH FACE in cold water**, cold bathing, cold drink, uncovering, walking, stimulants, spicies, pungent things, refreshing things, sour, **LEMONADE.**

They have **DREAMS** of death of **RELATIVE**, death of **FRIENDS**, dying, death, **BUSINESS** of the day, Fire( means you are heading into danger & need to be cautious), Intellectual, previous events.

They have **FEAR/DREAD of DEATH, MISFORTUNE(** something bad will happen), apoplexy.

**ANXIETY *makes them* WALK FAST.**

> **WALKING(** ***relief anxiety***), cold bathing, **CLOTHING PRESSURE**, morning, long after eating, perspiration, running, continued motion, short sleep, coffee, cold drink.

< **CONVERSATION**, reading, talking, **STIMULANTS, SMELL OF COFFEE**, sweet, tea, melon, fish, sour, snow air.

"***Palms -warm & perspiration***"

CHAPTER SIXTEEN

# GELSEMIUM

## *GELSEMIUM-( Yellow Jasmine)*

(HOT & THIIRSTLESS)

LEFT SIDED(1+)

FAST/SLOW FAST(3+)

SYCOSIS(1+)

**AILMENTS** from- **MENTAL** shock, reproach, grief, **FEAR, FRIGHT, EMOTIONAL EXCITEMENT,** embarrssment, humiliation, bad news( ***death of a child***).

**SLUGGISH CIRCULATION** leads to complete relaxation & prostration. Their senses of **DULL &BLUNTED.** They are **SPINELESS(** Lack of courage/daring/bravery). They grab bystander or furniture, or wants to be held. There is lack of confidence. (***stage fright***).

There is marked **SLOWNESS.**(They have difficulty in understanding, unable to think long, even apathy regarding their illness). There is confusion, dullness, indolence even sadness from/after masturbation. Even after sadness or grief they **CANNOT CRY.**

There is feeling of **TIREDNESS, HEAVINESS, WEAKNESS** & soreness.

They have **FEAR/DREAD** of speaking/appearing in public, of people( anthropophobia), **PUBLIC PLACES**, crowd, of being alone, **OF FAILURE, of FALLING**( Child hold on to mother), **before EXAMINATION**, of **GOING TO DOCTOR/DENTIST**, of dark, motion, of heart cease to beat unless constantly on the move, of water, of losing self control.

They have **AVERSION** to presence of other( so they avoid the sight of people), of **BEING DISTURBED**( Conversation), thinking, **BEING TOUCHED**, uncovering , motion, solitude.

< presence of others, mental exertion, **EXCITEMENT**, thinking of complaints, high place, **SPRING**, summer, tobacco.

> **COPIOUS flow of URINE**( vertigo, **EYE PAIN**, headache), binding/bandaging, perpiration, cold air, during menses, continued motion( riding in wagon or car).

They have **DESIRE** to be held, hold on, spitting, to be silent, open air.

Violent **DESIRE** driving them to **MASTURBATION**.

While **DREAMING** they do moaning, groaning & whining, falling on asleep. They **DREAM** of people, business, amorous, nightmares.

**"DULLNESS, DROWSINESS/SLEEPINESS/ TIREDNESS, EXHAUSTION,DIZZINESS/WHIRLING/ VERTIGINOUS. "**

CHAPTER SEVENTEEN

# GRAPHITES NATURALIS

## GRAPHITES NATURALIS-(BLACK LEAD)

*(CHILLY & THIRSTY)*

LEFT SIDED(3+),

PSORA(1+),

SYCOSIS(2+)

They donot have courage, **to have their own opinion** *(cowardice, timid, slowness of mind irresolute).* They feels unfortunate. They display a lack of good judgement *(they undertakes many things, maintain in nothing).* They face difficulty in thinking *(inability to calculate).* They have difficulty in concentration. They become **distress & unhappy from amenorrhoea.** They become discontented with everything ,with them.

They have marked **inclination/ pronencess to become amorous.** They intrude into sexual thoughts ***(lascious fancies)*** later sexual thought keep tormenting them. there is prostration of mind from mental exhaustion. They get offened & frightened easily. They **weep when anxious or sometimes *(even without cause).*** There is incontancy in mood *(variable).*

Their **FEAR > by weeping,**

They have **FEAR** of suffocation after by eating.

**FEAR** of crowd, people *(anthropophabias),* misfortune*(something bad will happen),* of evil, of business & **FEAR** lead to anxiety.

They have **AVERSION** to men, presence of others *(company),* mental work, uncovering, open air, cold air, **while thinking of meat, sweet *(sugar),*** fish, cooked food, coition.

< presence of others, comapny, consolation, conversation, **thinking of complaints, music,** bathing, washing deep breathing, **thought of food,** hunger, taliking, touch, uncovering.

> **weeping, eructation,** flatus, mucus secretion, **discharges, perspiration,** open air, mesmerism, riding in a wagon or a car, **warm milk.**

They **DESIRE -hot milk,**(warm drink), to be magnetized, to be silent, cold air *(so window must be open).*

They have **DREAM** of **misfortune,** danger from water,

accident( means-crashing of hopes),

fire(means-you are heading into danger & need to be catious),

disease *(fainting ,lethargy)* dead, **difficulties,** restless, *mental exertion, business of day,* dogs, cats. **Amorous,** historic, previous events, embarrasment, *excelling in mental work,*

striving *(means **struggle),***

water.

" **over weight,** unhealthy skin, **deformed nails, & delayed menses."**

"*what **puls** is at **puberty, graphites** is at **climacteric.***"

CHAPTER EIGHTEEN

# IPECACUANHA

## *IPECACUANHA-( Ipecac root)*

(THIRSTLESS)

"Oversensitive to BOTH extremes of TEMPERATURE"

Complaints/pain from LEFT to RIGHT.

RIGHT SIDE( 2+), LEFT SIDE( 1+)

PSORA(1+)

FAST PULSE(1+)

They are restless, impatience, irritable, anxious, confused & sad.

They are **ill-humour & weep DURING FEVER(heat).** They are indifferent to joy & pleasure. They are disrespectful, taunting to everything. They become hyper/ overcritical, become anger at little things, noise & about business. Chindrem cries, scream & are hard to please. They remain absorbed & buried in thoughts. Although they have very volatile, erratic, repulsive mood.

They have vivid & **FRIGHTFUL DREAMS.**

They have **AVERSION** to everything, mental work, open air, **SMELL OF FOOD**, fat & rich,

They have **DESIRE** to be carried, to be silent, indefinite, indistinct, inexpressible, FULL OF DESIRES, to weep all the time, cold air( window must be open), sweets.

> discharge, mucus secretion.

>**WALKING FAST**, while perspiration, **RAPID & HASTY DRINKING**, frozen food, sour fruit, ice, **PATSRY, DRY FOOD, SALAD, SMELL of FOOD**, sweet, open air.

"Threatened suffocation from mucuos ( RATTLING).

" **PROFUSE SALIVATION, CLEAN TONGUE, PERSISTENT NAUSEA & VOMITING**"

CHAPTER NINETEEN

# IRIS-VERSICOLOR

## *IRIS-VERSICOLOR-( Blue Flag)*

(THIRSTLESS)

SLOW PULSE (1+)

RIGHT SIDE(2+),LEFT SIDE(1+)

They have **DREAMS of "DISSECTING DEAD BODIES" OR SEEING DEAD BODIES**( Means you are disconnected from your feeling or devoid of emotions or it means that something that need to be buried is not yet, it's **been exposed, HAVE BEEN BROUGHT BACK UP**),

**DREAM** of **GRAVES, FALLING INTO GRAVE**( means **INSECURITY**, you are not stable & ought to feel safe or means difficult time),

**DREAM** of suffocation( means fear & anxiety),

**DREAM** of snake( means you consider your surrounding poisonous),

**DREAM** of fire( means you are heading into danger & need to be cautious),

**DREAM** of fight( means you genuinely wish to vent your rage by picking a fight),

**DREAM** that he had a FIT, amorous.

They have **AVERSION** to presence of others, company.

They have **FEAR/DREAD** of death, of impending disease/illness.

They are depressed with mental dullness. They laugh at their own action. Mostly discouraged. There is **SADNESS** before menses & during headache. ***Headache resulting from gastric derrangement***( mostly they have ***right sided headache*** with diarrhoea) .Headache < on coughing.

< presence of others, company, fruit, milk, farinacious food.

> when alone, eructation, flatus, **WALKING SLOWLY.**

**"FIRE/BURNING OF WHOLE GASTROINTESTINAL TRACT( from mouth to anus)."**

"***Diarrhoea after fruit or on alternate day***"

**"SALIVATION WHILE TALKING"**

CHAPTER TWENTY

# KALIUM BICHROMICUM

## KALIUM BICHROMICUM

*(CHILLY & THIRSTY)*

PSORA(1+),

SYCOSIS(1+),

SYPHILIS(2+),

FAST/SLOW PULSE(1+)

Core theme of this remedy is **"STRING"** of conscience.

Since childhood they are taught about ethics/ principles. They develop certain beliefs/ moral sense of right & wrong, which act as a guide to their behaviour. There after **they bind themselves *(STRING)* in certain routine** *(correct according to their moral teachings).* They have marked anxiety regarding their conscience. They are very timid/ slow.

They have delusion as if **committed a crime** or about to **commit acrime*(against conscience)*,** *or child was dead* (as a punishment).

They have intense **dislike**/ disgust **for life.** They **avoid human** society *(just talk to themselves). They are never in* *cheerful state, mostly in* ***bad mood,*** *discouraged, in discomfort. They get angry at little things sometimes.*

*They become irritable with* ***confusion*** *of mind, there is* ***difficulty in concentration*** *while reading & studying. They develop* ***in capacity & aversion*** *to business, mental & physical work peculiar thing is their irritability, sadness, headache, stomach pain & other mind symptoms are* ***better after eating*** *(so sometimes they over eat).*

> **eating,** occupied/ diverted, hot soup, mucus secretion especially head pain > tea.

They have **FEAR** of men, **people,** crowd, anthropophobia, dark, of being poisoned, ***of death before menses.***

They have **DREAMS** of danger, frightful, vivid, nightmares, fights. Most important is **SUFFOCATION**(*means* ***surrounded by controlling superior,*** *toxic people,* ***ungrateful friends & family****).*

They have **AVERSION** to **company,** mental work, reading, **tobacco smoking, meat,** fruit.

< **presence of others,** company, uncovering, **sight of food,** fruit, **chocolate, ice, tea,** physical exertion, heat of sun, hot weather.

- posterior nasal discharge/ catarrh - mostly **yellow-greenish** *(if suppressed leads to headache).*

***- right side*** *nose swelling/ right nose obstruction* ***smell lost*** */ or* ***putrid odour*** *from nose so constant inclination to blow nose.*

*" pain -* ***migratory in small spots & stringy discharge."***

CHAPTER TWENTY-ONE

# KALI-IODATUM

## *KALI-IODATUM*

(HOY & THIRSTY)

PSORA(1+)

SYCOSIS(2+)

SYPHILIS(3+)

PULSE FAST(1+)

**AILMENT** from- mental work, cold milk, hair cutting.

They are passionate, excitable, irritable & vindictive with sadness. They even weep from anxiety. They become anxious during sleep, after menses, after stool, from excitement. Although their anxiety get better by walking in open air. They become irritable after eating, or **towards CHILDREN**. They are hard hearted***/rough/harsh towards their family & children.*** ( ***indifference to their*** **CHILDREN**). They are voilent , obstinate, quarrelsome & restless.

They have great **AVERSION to CHILDREN** *whom they were devotedly attached*( **become BURDENSOME**), **AVERSION** to being touched, business, mental work, **COLD FOOD, COLD DRINK,** soup , fish, milk, food, coffee.

They **DESIRE -OPEN AIR, WALK, HOT & WARM DRINK**, stimulant, motion, uncovering, coffee.

They have **FEAR/DREAD** of evil, of suffocation, **evening( twilight)/ RETURN OF DAWN**, misfortune, they have fear with sadness.

They have **DREAMS of DANGER**, falling, murder, frightful, **BEING MURDERED**, nightmares.

> **WALKING ( Anxiety)**, eructation, flatus, uncovering, **COLD BATHING**, cold air, warm bed.

< **COVER( INTOLERANCE), HOT BATHING**, sea shore air, touch, summer season, change of temperature, pressure, warm room, long after eating, milk, cold drink, dry food.

"**GREEN DISCHARGE** from eyes, nose, ear, leucorrhoea, **EXPECTORATION**, from ulcer"

" Great disposition, for **HAIR TO CHANGE COLOUR & FALLOUT**"

CHAPTER TWENTY-TWO

# KREOSOTUM

## *KREOSOTUM*

(CHILLY & THIRSTY & LEFT SIDED)
FAST PULSE( 1+),SLOW PULSE( 1+),
PSORA(1+)
SYCOSIS(1+)

DARK complexion, TALL, LEAN with haemorrhagic DIATHESIS. They have irritability , excitability & restlessness **BEFORE MENSES.** Anxiety **DURING MENSES & during coition**. Anger at **MENSES** & at lilltle things. They have insanity/madness **AFTER BLEEDING/ HEMORRHAGE.** They have foregetfulness after epistaxis.

All secretion from mucous membrane/surface are excessivly acrid & corrosive.

Every emotion & exciting circumstance are attended with **THROBBING** all over the body, pulsation to the ends of the fingers.

They are sensistive to **MUSIC**, either excitement or sadness from music. Music causes weeping & palpitation. They are laughing/cheerful at night or during sleep. They are inclined to dwell on unpleasant things. Dissatisfied, despair & doubtful of recovery. There is sluggish, dullness, difficulty in thinking.( confusion of mind). Weakness of memory -**DURING SPEECH THEY REPEAT SAME THING AGAIN & AGAIN.**

They have **DELUSION** of worms, **BEETLES**, ringing of bells.

They have **DREAMS** of **BEETLES(means**- stress),

accidents, amorous,

**PENIS BREAKING OFF(means**-losing power, or desire to escape from the responsibilities)

, weeping, SNOW STORM, fire, murder, **DIRTY LINEN**(means- feeling betrayed),

dirt, involuntary urination at night, **HAVING TAKEN POISON**, laughing , growing things,

**BUGS**( means - fear & anxiety),

body becoming emaciated, **EMACIATION**, men following to violate her, being pursued by men to violate her, **RAPE**, being pursued for rape,

sore throat( means- ideas not fulling expressed),

disgusting, falling from height, disease, **POISONING**, being murdered.

They have **FEAR/DREAD** of **FASTING**, at thought of **RAPE/COITION**, impending disease. fear with anxiety.

They have **AVERSION** to **COITION** , open air, cooked ood, meat.

They have **DESIRE** to be carried, caressed, to be silent, warm & hot drinks, **SMOKED MEAT, SMOKEDFOOD.** They **DESIRE** impatiently for **many things** . But *throw them away & want something else then.*

< Music, uncovering, touch, hair combing, sour, meat, fruit, cold bathing, **FASTING.**

> Hot & warm food.

CHAPTER TWENTY-THREE

# MAGNESIUM CARBONICUM

## MAGNESIUM CARBONICUM

*(CHILLY & THIRSTY)*

PSORA(1+),

SYCOSIS(2+)

It is deep & long acting remedy.

losing flesh & **craving for meat/ pickled meat** in those who are tubercular or in those who are from tubercular family history.

**Anxious, tense, stressed or tenterhook & perspiration whole day** ,bitting nails.

They have **FEAR** - as if some accident would happen, all day.

There is anticipation before **going to physican/ dentist.**

Other **FEAR** are - of **robbers,** of misfortune, of death *(vomiting)* something bad will happen, accidents. All **FEAR** are with anxiety.

> **after going to bed,** evening, warmth of bed, alone, thinking of complaints, letting limbs hang down, stretching out affected part, walking fast, haemorrhage.

< company, presence of others, **uncovering, bathing, washing, undressing, working in water,** cabbage, sour fruit, **potatoes,** over eating, farinaceous food, talking touch, **vegetables,** milk.

They have **AVERSION** to **company,** to women, to everything, presence of others, **being touched, uncovering,** bread & butter, cooked food, spicy meat, **salad, vegetables,** green fruits, **milk.**

They have **DESIRE** to be silent, to travel, constipation, fruits, indistint doesnot know what, juicy things, meat, **picklet meat, vegetable,** milk, sour fruits.

They are **forgetful** after eating, there is difficulty of thinking while writing from mental exertion. They have difficulty in concentration, unable to read, confusion of mind. In **DELLUSION** they see thieves, of counting money, see dead person, incurable disease, will be murdered, They have unrefreshing sleep feel more tired on rising than retiring.

Their stool, skin odor, expectoration, vomiting, mouth odor, taste, perspiration **all smell sour,** infact they **DESIRE** for **sour** fruits.

They are mentally & physically sensitive to touch, to cold air *(still **DESIRE** for open air).* They get started when touched, from appoach of person timidity. They **weep aloud, with sobbing in sleep.** They cannot bear to be looked at irritable childrens, feels of **not being loved by parents, wife & friends.** They enjoy eating & often eat too much. They **even steal dainties/ whatever good to eat.**

They are discontented with everything. They are despair with pain, despair of recovery. They strike themselves knocking head against wall & things. They become talkative during drunkenness state, they even talks to themselves.

They have **DREAMS** of flower, fruit, lottery, fish, money *(all means feeling of happiness, growth, progress, prosperity).*

**DREAM** of **unsuccessful in finding way to** his own **house** *(means no place to rest or seeking stability in life).*

**DREAM** of **being soaked in pain** *(means feeling of helplessness).*

**DREAM** of **child bathing in boiling water** *(means decision in life harshly criticized).*

**DREAM** of **unsuccessful in dressing** for a event *(means nervousness, fear of failure).*

**DREAM***of* **unsuccessful efforts** *(means nervousness anxiety).*

**DREAM** of grave *(means fear of having your personal feeling & private thoughts revealed).*

**DREAM** of robbers *(means feeling powerless).*

**DREAM** of **hair falling out** *(means fear worries & anxiety).*

**DREAM** of **burnt breast***(means insecurity or loneliness).*

**DREAM** of **burnt back***(means feeling as if someone is trying to cause you trouble).*

**DREAM** of beggar *(means emptiness with in you, insecurity).*

**DREAM** of **fight with robbers** *(means rush to succeed without thorough thinking about your path).*

**DREAM** of **thrown into grave** *(means feeling stuck in some aspect of your life).*

**DREAM** of journey *(means you have to discipline your habits).*

**DREAM** of flood *(means overwhelming emotions).*

**DREAM** of **danger from water**, wedding, water, **unsuccessful of talking**, storm, quarrels, that he had a fit, dead relative, out burst of passion, **lost at home**, Historic, **obliged to dressing hair in company**, difficulties, hair, funerals, embarrassment, disease, epilepsy, contraband, smugling, didnot wish to make up clothes, **cheek burnt,** of being thirsty,

**DREAM** of being arrested *(means powerless feeling).*

**DREAM** of fire *(means you are heading toward danger, need to be cautious).*

**DREAM** of dancing *(means expressing yourself to the fullest)*

**DREAM** of masks *(means feeling of insecurity).*

**DREAM** of lost in forest *(means feeling of confusion, or lack of support in your life).*

During case taking **DREAMS** of the patient **are message for stored or hidden / information.**

**"discharge of prostatic fluid when passing flatus."**

" pain in head **as if hair were pulled."**

CHAPTER TWENTY-FOUR

# MEZERUM

## MEZERUM-( SPURGE OLIVE )

*( CHILLY & THIRSTY)*

LEFT SIDED(3+), RIGHT SIDED(2+),
PSORA(1+),
SYCOSIS(2+),
SYPHILIS(2+),
FAST PULSE(2+), SLOW PULSE(1+)

I had a case of *(teenage girl)* with some pustular eruptions on scalp, dandruf & hairfall. Her hair were stick/ glued matted together, due to pustular discharge with violent pain & itching. She was irritable, confused, moody & absent minded finally got cured with MEZERUM.

They had DREAMS of **difficulties with journey** *(means difficulties with **journey/ phase of life,** like **seperation** and all),*

**DREAM** of **excrescence's** disease, body part, back, breast covered with warts, **WARTS** *(means unresolved feeling of anxiety & **separation** or struggling with your **individuality & independence** in some **aspect of their relationships).***

***DREAM*** *of* ***cat*** (means you feel surrounded by malicious people).

**DREAM** of falling from high place, nightmares, confused, amorous, ludicrous, pleasant.

They have **DELUSION** as if they have **WARTS,** as if they are poor, of everything is dead.

They have **DEASIRE** to **pull their hair, to wash face in cold water,** company, to rest, coffee, cold drink, mustard.

They have **AVERSION** to **hat, to being touched, solitude,** to mental work, to everything, bathing, motion, meat.

They have **FEAR** of being **alone,** exertion, misfortune.

**FEAR** leads to anxiety. They look for hours at window with `**dull senses,** weak memory. They dwell of past disagreeable occurences. They remain **dissatisfied with themselves,** surrounding & everythings. There is feeling of **loathing of life.**

They are **sad when alone, about little things.** There is weary of life. They get **angry at littlethings** or without any cause or from headache.

Due to brooding, they have **difficulty of thinking** (dullness while reading). So they become indifferent while reading, to pleasure & to everything.

They are sensitive to pain *(weeping with pain).*

They become quarrelsome *(reproaches others)* confused mind.

< **solitude,** conversation, laughing, **talk of others,** uncovering, undressing, bathing, washing, laughing, touching hair.

> *(dullness, confusion & anxiety get* ***better by eating)*** *occupied/ diverted,* ***bathing face*** (affected part).

**"ECZEMA & ITCHING ERRUPTIONS AFTER VACCINATION"**

CHAPTER TWENTY-FIVE

# NATRUM CARBONICUM

**NATRUM CARBONICUM**

*(THIRSTY)*

*(sensitive to both extremes of temperature)*

RIGHT SIDED(2+),

PSORA(2+),

SYCOSIS(1+),

FAST PULSE(2+)

They have **DREAM** of **difficulties on/ with journey, unsuccessful** *(efforts)*,

**journey on horseback/** horse riding( means- strong drive towards your goals),

danger from water,

**having ears cut off/ cutting**(means- you have had enough of listening to others & you want to do your own things or simply to have some peace for a while),

**being pulled by nose**( means- completely under someone's control),

being stabbed, stab his antagonist, knives, **dead friends,** funerals, fire, wedding, **wedding with two**

**women,confused,** flood, water, thunderstorm, soldier, riots, remorse, quarrel, nightmare, murder, ghost, entertainment, **amorous,** many, long parties, people, recalling things long forgotten.

They are shy ,**never reveal their grief** & sorrow. They **hate socializing due** to weary of life. They are **introvert/** keep self- analysing or pondering too much. They are **indifferent** to relations, to pleasure, to money making, to society, to children, **to own family.** They are **no longer on friendly terms** with family, friends & society.

They are **constantly occupied with sad thought,** discouraged & dissatisfied with everything. They get frightened & offended easily. There is depression & sadness even from errors of diet.

They have **DELUSION of doing nothing wrong** or **they do everything wrong & cannot be succeed,** surrounding by soldiers, pursued by soldiers or enemies, of wedding.

They do have sympathy, compassion & always **ready to help others.** Although they do not want **consolation** for themselves.

There is dullness/ confusions/ prostration of mind from mental exertion. Mental work become impossible for them. They are **unable to reflect from studying** especially **young people, who have weakmemory for what they have study.** They have irritability when reading , feel dullness while reading inability to calculate very confused behaviour.

They have difficult & slow comprehension & lack of confidence, irresolute, mental depression leading to mental weakness. They have **inconsolable,** intolerable melancholy.

They have lascivious fancies, greedy gut. They **enjoy eating & often eat too much.** Along with food they take lot of water. They have bad assimilation, acid dyspepsia &stomach troubles.

They have **FEAR of people**, men ,company, crowd, robber, thunder strom, noise, music, of death, misfortune, of impending disease.

They have **AVERSION to husband, family members,** to all person, **of intimate friends,** presence of other, company, mental work, uncovering, open air, coffee, honey, milk, **meat during dinner.**

They **DESIRE solitude *(when sad)*** death, nibble, to strike, to be **silent,** potatoes, sweets, cold drink, **oftobacco smoking after dinner.**

> **alone,** magnetized, occupied/ diverted, **darkness.**

< **consolation, presence of others, intimate friends,** company, talk of others, mental exertion, music, uncovering, bathing, washing, over eating, dry food, farinacious food, heavy food, honey, milk, pears, pepper, sour, vinegar, **spring,** summer, **touch, talking, sun.**

CHAPTER TWENTY-SIX

# PODOPHYLLUM PELTATUM

***PODOPHYLLUM PELTATUM-( MAY APPLE)***

(CHILLY & THIRSTY)

RIGHT SIDED( 2+)

PULSE SLOW(2+)

PSORA( 1+)

Pain/complaints appear **suddenly**.

**AILMENTS** since summer season.

They have **DREAD/FEAR** of impending **DISEASE, of DEATH.**

They have **DELUSION** of having a Heart disease, of being sick, is going to have **HEART DISEASE & DIE**.

They have **DELIRIUM** That they will **DIE** & cannot be helped.

They become despair/anxious about salvation, especially in **TWILIGHT( evening)**. & become restless at **NIGHT.** crying/howling/moaning( in children , in dentition, during sleep, during cough). Screaming/ shouting with pain.

They become excessively **IRRITABLE, EXCITABLE & TALKATIVE**( in liver trouble, during chill & heat, during sleep).

They worry about Business/work. with prostration of mind they become forgetful ( **DURING HEAT & CHILL).**

They have **AVERSION** to milk, food, **SMELL OF FOOD.**

They have **DESIRE** to bite, to be carried( over shoulder), to breath deep, cold drink, sour.

> evening, **LYING ON ABDOMEN**( In pregnancy also)

< drinking, physical exertion, cabbage, cooked food, fruit, sour fruit, oyster, **SMELL OF FOOD**, summer season, **WARM AIR & WEATHER, HOT WEATHER.**

"**GRINDING TEETH** , sleep with **EYE HALF CLOSED**"

I have used this remedy many times with superb results **for joints pain POST CHIKUNGUNYA FEVER** & patients revealed that 80% of their pain get over within first 24 hours after PODO 1M.

CHAPTER TWENTY-SEVEN

# SARASPRILLA OFFICINALIS

**SARASPARILLA** -(WILD LIQUARICE)
(CHILLY & THIRSTY/THIRSTLESS)
RIGHT SIDED(3+)
PSORA (2+)
SYCOSIS (2+)
SYPHILIS (2+)

They have **DREAD/FEAR** that they will not recover (during climacteric period), of shaking/trembling, before sleep, of bathing(even **aversion** too). Although they have **AVERSION** to everything.

They scream/shout before urination. There is **SAND** in urine/stool/diaper.

They have very changeable /variable/ alternating mood. They feel unfortunate, become irritable(during menses), weep (before menses), get easily offended.They become sad during headache/from pain/from masturbation/ pollution. They develop indifference to pleasure.They remain buried in thoughts(especially on past disagreeable occurence/recall old grievances). Disgust/dissatisfied with everything. They remain doubtful of their recovery (during climacteric period) & when mood changes , they become

**CHEERFUL.**

They have **DELUSION-as if they are FRIENDLESS, BODY is brittle**, see dead person.

They have difficulty in concentration/thinking, confusion, dullness, sluggishness.

They have **DREAMS** - of accidents, amorous, business,

**STOOL/EXCREMENT**(means reflection of freedom),

dead relative, disaster, frightful, white ghost,

**fighting with ghost**( means you are ready to face ,regardless of the outcome),

spinning( means- situation where you have no control),

previous events, falling, mental exertion, *sleigh rides,* vexatious,

**SPIDERS**( means you are afraid of something & your mind is trying to avoid it),

They have **DESIRE** to be silent,open air, refreshing things(cold food, cold drink, juicy things)

Their sexual desire somtimes *disturb their sleep.*

< conversation, talking,thinking of complaints, **clothing(external throat)**, cold bathing, washing,thought of food, warm food & drink, dry food, wet weather, spring, beginning of motion.

>**loosing clothing**, darkness, while fasting , long after eating, cold food, dry weather, haemorrhage,walking.

" Eruptions following hot weather & VACCINATION"

I have used it many times it give superb results especially for " severe pain at end of urination".

CHAPTER TWENTY-EIGHT

# SABINA

### ***SABINA***

(HOT & THIRSTY)

RIGHT SIDED(2+), LEFT SIDED(2+)

PSORA(1+),

SYCOSIS(2+)

In patients who menstruate very early in life. There is sense of fullness in all veins of the body, with pulsation. They are **SENSIIVE** to noise( music). They become **SAD & DEPRESSED** from music. They even **WEEP** from music, during sleep, & after anger. They are **JOYLESS** & discouraged, , with **QUIET**, disposition( **RESERVED**). They have anxiety about future.

Sometimes they are lascivious, lustful, nymphomanic, shamless & restless.

They have **FEAR/DREAD of THREATINING ABORTION**, from **MUSIC**, of evil, mostly with anxiety.

They have **AVERSION** to **MUSIC**, jesting( joke), work, to coition.

They have **DREAMS** of quarrels, striving, **MEN KILLED BY FALLING FROM HIGH PLACE**, being busy, anger, unsuccessful in business, full of invention, intellectual, excelling in mental work, physical & mental exertion, falling, business of the day.

They have **DESIRE** to be silent, magnetized, open air( window must be open), **COFFEE, COFFEE BEANS, REFRESHING THINGS(** Juicy things, **LEMONADE**, cold dink, sour), milk.

< Consolation, **MUSIC**, motion, cloudy rainy weather, touch, warm bed, milk.

> magnetized, cold air, pressure, after perspiration, flatus, walking fast, while fasting.

" **Menses partly fluid & PARTLY CLOTTED( DARK), + COLDNESS of hands**"

CHAPTER TWENTY-NINE

# SELENIUM

### *SELENIUM*

(HOT & THRSTY)

LEFT SIDED(3+)

PSORA(1+)

SYCOSIS(2+)

I have seen many cases where patients complaints of **SEMEN DISCHARGE while DEFECATING** or while doing any **JERKY ACTIVITY**( Like kicking the two wheeler).

Their all mental & nervous symptoms are **worse AFTER COITION**. There is general weakness **AFTER COITION**. Dissatistication, irritability, ill humor, confusion of mind, difficulty in thinking, dullness, sluggishness, sadness, prostration of mind **AFTER COITION/from pollution.** Mental work become impossible **after SEXUAL EXCESS.**

Still they have **SEXUAL thought, LASCIVIOUS fancies, LUSTFUL behaviour with IMPOTENCY.** This show they have strong sexual desire, but is physically impotent. All impaction, comprehension & understanding. make them incable for busines( senses becomes dull & blunted).

They **DREAM of LONG FORGOTTEN THINGS,** previous events, **AMOROUS**, historic,

robbers( means- you feel insecure &weak),
anger, cruelty, misfortune, of liquid with thirst.

They **FEAR/DREAD** of crowd, people , of men, of occupation, work, of impending disease, apoplexy.

They have **AVERSION** to company, presence of others, **INTIMATE FRIENDS**, salt, **TEA.**

They **DESIRE**- ***coffee, alcoholic drink before*** **MENSES.**

< Presence of others, intimate friends, company, talking, mental exertion, touching hair, combing, open air, fruit, **LEMONADE**, salt, sugar, **TEA**, wine.

> rest, standing, darkness, perspiration, haemorrhage, warm air.

" **FALLING OUT OF HAIR** from **EYEBROW**, whiskers, beard, head, **GENITALS** & Almost all over the body."

CHAPTER THIRTY

# TARENTULA

## TARENTULA

(CHILLY & THIRSTY)

FAST PULSE(3+)

PAIN APPEAR SUDDENLY(2+)

When touched ,they are **VOILENTLY ANGER**. They **THREATEN TO KILL**( threatening speech). Disobedience, they **REFUSE TO EAT**. With increased strength ,they become **DESTRUCTIVE,WILD**, hysterical, they **STRIKE** their head with hands, tear their hair, tear things, they even **STRIKE** their friends from anger.throw things away. They get excited from music , **DANCING**, singing, they even start **WEEPING** from music, when anything refused, from contradiction, hysterical ,causeless.

They are conscious about unnatural state of their mind. They torment ( torture) themselves. with increased restlessness they are compelled to **WALK RAPIDLY** & talk excessivly. Their anxiety get better by excercise( so they keep themself fruitlessly busy) They keep on immoderatly laughing, mocking, singing untill their voice become hoarse & exhausted. ***When there are no observer there is*** **no HYSTERIA, WHEN ATTENSION is directed TOWARD**

**THEM they begin to FAKE their illness/sickness/ fainting.**

They are shameless( expose), most of the time they put their **FINGER IN MOUTH**. They are having sexual mania both in men & women. showing lascivious , lustful & sexual behaviour. They become hypochondriac after masturbation. pruritus vulvae leads to nymphomania. pruritus vulvae mostly after menses. They have sadness **AS IF IN FAULT**, or after sexual excitement.

They have **DELUSION as if BEING SICK**, going to be assaulted, being insulted, or **LEGS ARE CUT OFF.**

Theyhave **DREAM of FALLING FROM HORSE**(means- you need to regain control of your life), danger, death , dead bodies, horses,

**BEINGPURSUED BY BULLS(means-** your irresistibility or stubbornness),

by animals & wild animals, misfortune, contempt, insults, long, water, sad.

They have **FEAR/DREAD of BEING ASSAULTED**( So desire to hide), water, touch, noise, music, during **WALKING RAPIDLY**, misfortune( something bad will happen), **OF TYPHOID FEVER,** of evil, of eating, of death, of impending disease, causeless, fear of people, of others approaching them.

They have **AVERSION** to answer, to **COLOUR**( black, red, yellow, gree, blue), touched, **CHOCOLATE**, food, meat, coition.

They have **DESIRE** to bite themself, for business, to hide, **TO THREATEN TO KILL, to LAUGH**, play, **PULL ONE'S HAIR**, to be Silent, to walk, to **SHOW BEING SICK**, mental work, open air, bathing, **ASHES, SAND,** cold drink, indigestible( chalk, clay,slate) raw food, salt, spices.

< consolation, music, coition, presence of stranger, **SEEING OTHER'S IN TROUBLE**, physical exertion, cold drink, butter, fat, fruit.

> **EXCERCISE(RELIEF ANXIETY) , EATING( relief discouragment)**, eating , music, **COITION( relief IRRITATION), OCCUPIED/DIVERTED**,eructation, haemorrhage, darkness, flatus, motion, slow walking.

"Remedy for **PAIN OF DEATH**, soothes the **LAST agony or STRUGGLE**( similar to Arsenic Album)"

CHAPTER THIRTY-ONE

# HOT & THIRSTLESS

**APIS,** allium cepa, ***arg-n***, bry, calad, led, ***lyc,*** nat-m,***op***, **PULS**, thuja.

# HOT & THIRSTY

***all-c,*** aloe, apis, **ARG-N, BRY,** ***fl-ac,*** **IOD,** ***kal-i, lach,*** lyc, **NAT-M,** nat-s, **OP,** pic-ac, plat, puls, **SECALE, SULPH,** ***thuja.***

CHAPTER THIRTY-TWO

# CHILLY & THIRSTLESS

***agn***, am-c, ars, ***bell***, ***camph***, canth, caps, caust, chel, **CHINA**, cocc, **COLCH**,***con***, ***cycl***, ***ferr***,HELL, hep, ign, kal-ar, ***kalic-carb***, mur-ac, nat-carb, nitric-ac, **NUX-M**, nux- v, oxal-ac, phos, **PH-AC**,**SABAD**, sars, ***sepia***, spig, ***staph***, stram, valer.

# CHILLY & THIRSTY

**ACON**, agar, agn, **ARS**, alum, aur, ***bar-c, bell***, **CALC-C**, ***camp, canth, carb-v***, **CAUST**, **CHAM**, ***chel***, **CHIN**, ***cocc, colch, con***, cycl, ***dulc***, graph, **HELL**, ***hep, hyosc***, kali-ar, ***kali-bi, kali-carb, kalm***, kreos, ***mag-c***, ***nat-c, nitric-ac***, nux-m, ***nux-v***, ox-ac, **PHOS**, ph-ac, ***plb, podo***, psor, ***ran-b***, rhod, **RHUS-T**, ruta, sabad, sars, sepia, **SIL**, spig, staph, **STRAM**, stront, sul-ac, ther, ***zinc.***

CHAPTER THIRTY-THREE

# HOT REMEDIES

***Aesc-h, all-c, aloe***, ambra, **APIS**, **ARG-NIT**,***asf, aur-iod, aur m,*** bar-iod, ***bry, calad, calc-iod, calc-sulph, cocc-cati,*** comoc, ***crocus***, ***dros***, fer-iod, **FLUOR-AC**, ***grat, ham***, **IOD**, **KALI-IOD, KALI-SULPH**, ***lach, led, lil-t, lyc***, **NAT-MUR**, **NAT-SUL**, niccol, ***op***, picric-acid, **PLAT**, ptelia, **PULS,SABINA, SECALE**, ***spong, sul, sul-iod***, thuj, tuber, ustil, ***vespa***, viburn.

CHAPTER THIRTY-FOUR

# CHILLY REMEDIES

abrot, acet-ac, ***acon, agar, agn, alumen, alum,Al-ph, alum-sil, am-c,*** apoc,***arg-m,*** **ARS**, ars-s-fl, asar, ***aur,*** aur-ars, aur-sulp, ***bad,*** **BAR-C,*****bar-m, bell,*** benz-ac, ***borax, brom***, cadm, ***calc-ars,*** **CALC-C,** ***calc-fl,*** **CALC-PH,** ***calc-sil,*** camph, ***canth,*****CAPS,** ***carb-an, carb-veg, carbn-sul,*** card-m, ***cauloph,*** **CAUST,** ***cham, chel,*** **CHINA,** ***chin-a, cimic, cistus, cocc, coff, colch, con, cycl,*** **DULC,** ***euphras,*** **FERR,** ***ferr-ars,form,*** **GRAPH,** guaj, ***hell, helon,*****HEP,** ***hyosc,*** **HYPER,** ***ign,*** **KALI-ARS,** ***kali-bich,*** **KALI-CARB,** ***kali-chlor,*** kali-phos, ***kali-sil, kalm,kreos, lac-defl,*** **MAGN-CARB, MAGN-PHOS,** ***mang,*** **MOSCH,** ***mur-ac, nat-ars, natr-carb,*** **NITRIC-ACID,** ***nux-m,*** **NUX-VOM,** ***oxal-ax, petrol,*** **PHOS,** ***phos-ac, plb, pod,*** **PSOR, PYROGEN,RAN-B,** rheum,***rhodo,*** **RHUS, RUMEX,** ***ruta,*** **SABAD,** ***sars,*** **SEPIA, SIL, SPIG,** ***stann***, staph, stram, **STRONT,** ***sul-ac, therid***, valer, viol-t, ***zinc.***

CHAPTER THIRTY-FIVE

# THIRSTLESS REMEDIES

**ANT-T, APIS, CHI, COLCH, GELS, HELL, MENY, NUX-M, PH-AC, SABAD.**

***aesc, acon, am-m, ant-c, arg-n, ars, bell, bov, camph, con, cycl, dios, ferr, hydr-ac, ip, kali-c, lyc, mang, olnd, op, samb, sep, staph.***

agar, aal-c, am-c, ambr, bry, bufo, calad, canth, caps, caust, chel, cimic, cocc, cor-r, crot-t, hep, ign, iris, kali-p, led, merc-c, mez, mur-ac, nat-c, nat-m, nat-s, nit-ac, nux-v, ox-ac, petr, phos, plat, sars, spig, stram, sulph, tab, thuj, valer, verat.

CHAPTER THIRTY-SIX

# THIRSTY REMEDIES

**ACON, ARG-N, ARS, BRY, CALC, CALC-S, CAPS, CAUST, CHAM, CHIN, DIG, EUP-PER, HELL, IOD, MERC, NAT-M, OP, PHOS, RHUS-T, SEC, SIL, STRAM, SULPH, TARRNT, VERAT.**

***all-c, am-m, anac, ant-c, apoc, arn, ars-i, bapt, bar-c, bar-m, bell, berb, bol, bor, calc-ar, camph, canth, carb-ac, carb-v, chel, chin-a, chin-s, cic, cimic, cina, coc-c, cocc, colch, coloc, con, croc, crot-c, crot-h, cupr, dros, culc, ferr-p, fl-ac, hep, hyos, kali-bi, kali-c, kali-i, kali-p, kali-s, kal,m, lach, laur, led, mag-c, merc-c, merc-i-f, mez, nat-a, nat-c, nat-p, nit-ac, nux-v, plb, podo, ran-b, raph, rat ther, thuj, verat-v, zinc.***

aesc, aeth, agar, agn, all-s, aloe, alum, am-c, ant-t, apis, aur, cor-r, glon, graph, ip, kreos, lil-t, lyc, mag-m, mag-s, mur-ac, naja, nat-s, nux-m, ox-ac, petr, ph-ac, pic-ac, plat, psor, puls, rhod, rob, ruta, sabad,samb, sang, sars, sel, sep, spig, stann, staph, stront, sul-ac, tab.

CHAPTER THIRTY-SEVEN

# WARM FOOT

**CHAM, PULS, SUPH.**

***apis, arund, caust, cocc, gon,kali-bi, lyc, nat-s, nux-v, petr, psor, ruta, sec, sep, sil.***

acon, agar, ang, arn, ars-h, ars, aster, brom, bufo, calad, calc, camp, carb-an, carb-s, carb-v, cimic, coff, coloc, crot-h, cub, hyos, ign, kali-ar, kali-chl, kali-i, lach, laur, led, merc, mez, mill, morph, nat-c, nat-m, nat-p, nit-ac, par, ph-ac, phos, phy, ptel, rhem, rhus-t, rhus-v, spig, spong, stann, staph, sumb, til, vip, zinc.

# WARM SOLE

**LYC, SULPH.**

***calc, carl, cham,cocc, ferr, graph, lach, lil-t, manc, nat-c, nux-v, petr, ph-ac, phos, puls, sang, sanic, sep, sil.***

am-m, apoc, ars-s-f, bell, berb, carb-s, carb-v, clem, coc-c, cub, dulc, eup-per, ferr-p, fl-ac, kali-n, lith, mang, med, mur-ac, nat-m, nit-ac, nux-m, ox-ac, plb, psor, samb, sars, spig, stann, stram, verat, zinc.

CHAPTER THIRTY-EIGHT

# COLD FOOT

**ANT-C, ANT-T, APIS, ARS, ARS-I, AUR, BELL, BROM, CALC, CARBN-S, CAUST, CHIN, CON, CUPR, DIG, DROS, FERR, FERR-I, GRAPH, IOD, IP, KALI-AR, KALI-C, KALI-N, KALI-P, KALI-S, KREOS, LACH, LYC, MENY, MERC, NAJA, NAT-C, NAT-M, NIT-AC, PAR, PETR, PH-AC, PHOS, PULS, RHOD, RUTA, SEP, SIL, SQUIL, STRAM, SULPH, THUJ.**

*acon, am-br, am-c, anac, arg-n, arn, asar, bar-c, bov, cact, camph, canth, caps, carb-ac, carb-an, carb-v, caul, cham, chel, chin-ar, cimx, cina, cist, cocc, colch, crot-c, crot-t, elaps, ferr-p, gels, glon, hell, hep, lycps, mang, med, merc-c, mur-ac, nat-p, nat-s, nux-m, nux-v, ox-ac, phyt, pic-ac, plb, podo, psor, rhus-t, sabin, samb, sars, stann, stront, tarent, verat-v, verat, zinc.*

# COLD SOLE

***coloc, nit-ac, sulph.***

acon, ars, caust, chel, chin-s, colch, hyper, laur, lith-c, merc, nux-v.

CHAPTER THIRTY-NINE

# WARM HAND

**AGAR, BELL, CHEL, LACH, LED, LYC, NAT-C, NIT-AC, NUX-M, OP, PHOS, PULS, RHOD, SEP, STAPH, SULPH, TARAX.**

***ant-t, bar-c, carb-v, cham, cycl, fl-ac, glon, graph, guai, iod, kali-bi, kali-c, kali-p, lil-t, mag-c, nux-v, petr, ph-ac, plan, psor, sabad, spig, stann.***

# WARM PALM

**ACON, ASAR, BRY, IP, LACH, MUR-AC, PHOS, SULPH.**

***bor, calc, eup-per, ferr, fl-ac, gels, lil-t, lyc, med, nux-v, petr, samb, sep, stann.***

CHAPTER FORTY

# COLD HAND

**ARS, ARS-I, AUR, CALC-AR, CALC-P, CAMPH, CARB-V, CHEL, CHIN, CYCL, FERR, FERR-I, FERR-P, GRAPH, IOD, IP, KALI-AR, KALI-C, KALI-P, LACH, LYC, LYCPS, MENY, MERC, MUR-AC, NAT-C, NAT-M, NAT-P, NUX-M, OLND, PETR, PH-AC, PULS, RUTA, SABIN, SAMB, SEC, SEP, SULPH, VERAT**

***acon, agar, ant-t, apis, arg-n, arn, bar-c, bar-m, bell, bov, brom, cact, calc, carb-ac, carb-an, carb-s, caust, cedr, chin-a, chin-s, cina, croc, crot-c, cupr, dig, dros, eup-per, gels, hell, led, mang, med, mez nit-ac, nux-v, op, ox-ac, pall, phos, phyt, pyrog, rhus-t, rob, sang, stram, sumb, tab, thuj, verat-v, zinc.***

# COLD PALM

acon, dig, hyos, jatr.

CHAPTER FORTY-ONE

# MIASM-REMEDIES

## PSORA-

**PSOR, SULPH,**

***agar, ant-c, ars-i, bar-c, calc, calc-p, car-an, carb-v, cupr, hep, kali-c, lyc, mag-c, mag-m, merc-, murx, nat-c, nat-m, nit-ac, petr, sars, sil.***

# SYCOSIS-REMEDIES

**ARG-M, ARG-N, KALI-S, MED, NAT-S, NIT-AC, SEP, STAPH, THUJ.**

*agar, anan, apis, ars, aster, aur-m, bar-c, benz-ac, calc, caust, dulc, ferr, fl-ac, graph, iod, kali-i, kalm, lach, lyc, mang, merc-c, merc-s, mez, nat-m, nat-p, phyt, sars, sec, sel, sil, sulph.*

# SYPHILIS-REMEDIES

**ARS-I, AUR, AUR-M, AUR-M-N, CALC-F, KAL-I, KALI-S, LAUR, MERC, MERC-C, MERC-I-F, MERC-I-R, NIT-AC, PHYT, SIL, SYPH.**

***ars-s-f, ars, asaf, calc-i, calc-s, carb-an, cinnb, con, fl-ac, hep, iod, kali-ar, kali-bi, kali-chl, lach, led, mez, ph-ac, phos, sars, staph, sul-i, sulph, thuj.***

arg-m, bad, benz-ac, carb-v, clem, cor-r, crot-h, guaj, petr.

# Conclusion+dream Repertory

## *CONCLUSION*

In these 30 **remedies**. I have mentioned *various* **DREAMS** ...like

**DREAMS** of-accidents( ars, graph, nux-v),

Being pursued by wild animals or horses( alum),

Journey by water full of snakes( alum),

Drowning(alum, ign, kali-c, lyc, merc, sil, verat,zinc),

Falling( bell, thuja, hep, merc, puls, sars, sulph),

Funerals( alum, mag-c, nat-c),

Marriages(alum, mag-c, ),

Danger( ars, hep, lach),

Snakes(arg-n, alum, iris, kali-c, kalm, lach, sep, sil),

Being bitten by snakes( arg-n),

Fishes( arg-n, kali-c, mag-c),

Insects(arg-n),

Putrid water(arg-n),

Hunger( arg-n, bry,calc, ign) ,

Danger from water( graph, mag-c, ars, merc, nat-c, sulph),

Dead bodies( calc, thuja),

Black water( ars),

Cats(arn, ars, calc-p, graph, hyos, mez, nux-v, op, puls, thuj),

Difficulties( ars, graph, mag-c, phos, alum, ant-t, bell, rhus-t, sep),

Unsuccessful( calc, cham, choc, ign, mag-c, nat-c, op, ph-ac),

Sick people( calc, ign, staph),

Murder(arn, kros, nat-m, sil, staph),

Fire( hep, mag-c, ars, bell, calc-p, kreos, nat-m, phos, rhus-t, sulph),

Meeting friends( calc-p),

Robbers( alum, mag-c, nat-m, arn, aur, kali-c, merc, sil, zinc),

Journey( apis, calc-p, crot-h, lach, mag-c, nat-c, op, rhus-t, sil, tub),

Water(all-c, ars, bell, ferr, graph, kali-c, lyc, merc, sil),

Sea( all-c, chin ),

Injuries( ant-c, chin, choc, phos),

Being stabbed( chin, nat-c, op),

Dispute for money(chin),

Being buried alive(arn, ign),

Falling into water(ferr, ign, iod, merc, ph-ac),

Of being murdered(kreos, lach, ign, lyc, merc, phos, sil, zinc),

Of being beaten(kal-c, nat-m),

Of children being beaten(kali-c, nat-m),

Quarrel with dead relatives(kali-c),

Suffocation(arn, iris, kali-bi, kali-c),

Calling out for help(kal-c),

Riots(bry, con, kali-c, lyc, merc, nat-c, nat-m, phos, puls),

Of stabbing others( lach),

Full of inventions(apis, lach, sabin),

Death of friend(con, fl-ac, lach),

Being accused of theft(choc, lach),

Urinating(kreos, sep, bell, lyc, sulph),

Swimming(bell, iod, lyc, rhus-t),

Boat foundering( alum, lyc, sil),

Disease-pain(med, bry, lyc),

Fight(all-c, ferr, nat-m, staph, stram),

Flying(apis, bell, lyc),

Flood(mag-c, merc, nt-c, sil),

Falling from height(thuj, kreos, mez, sulph),

Shooting( merc, hep, spong),

Rebellion(merc),

Firearms(merc),

Swallowing pins(merc),

Being bitten by animals(dogs)( sulph, calc, merc, verat),

Being taken as a prisoner( nat-m),

Crime(nat-m, nit-ac),

Teeth pulled out( nat-m),

Being to die( nit-ac, sil),

Someone is lying under him( nit-ac),

Being pursued by dogs & cats( nux-v, sil. verat),

Cruelty(nat-m, nux-v, sel, sil),

Falling out teeth( nux-v),

Worms(am-c, nux-v, phos),

Blood( phos, rhus-t),

Haemorrhages(phos),

Defecation in open( staph, phos),

Black dogs( arn, puls),

Black animals,

Naked men(puls),

Gold((puls) ,

Money(alum, mag-c, phos, puls, zinc),

Rowing(rhus-t),

Running(bell),

Ascending(rhus-t),

Climbing(rhus-t),

Body or face disfigured(sep),

Fight with ghost(sars, sep, sil),

Going & lost in forest( sep),

Rat , mice(sep),
Rape(kreos, sep),
Being pursued must run backward(sep),
Being burn(sep),
Of youth time(sil),
Past events( sil, am-c, calad, chin, ferr, nat-c, sulph),
Storm(ars, sil, mag-c),
Being pursued by ghost( sil),
Having been betrayed(sil),
Shameful( alum, am-c, arn, con, led, staph, tub),
Other seeing him naked while bathing or defecating(staph),
Fire coming down from the heaven( sulph),
Being crushed( sulph),
Danger of death( bell, sulph, thuj) .
BEING SHOT(bell),
GYMNASTICS(bell),
BEING PURSUED BY GIANTS(bell),
SHOOTING(merc, hep, spong),
GIANTS( bell, lyc),
VERMIN( nux-v, alum, am-c, bell, phos, sep, sil),
BATTLE( all-c, bell, bry, ferr, hyos, sil, thuj),
WALKING(bell, canth, elaps, med, nat-c, rhus-t),
SWIMMING IN WATER( bell, iod, lyc, rhus-t),
RUNNING(bell)
RIDING IN A CARRIAGE(bell),
ASSASSINS(bell) ,
HOUSEHOLD( bry, bell),
BEING BUSY(bry, apis, bell, camph, canth, hyos, ign, lach, led, lyc, phos, sabad, sabin, sep),
HIGH WAVES(all-c),
CLIFF(all-c),
FALLING INTO WELL(all-c),

SEA STORM(all-c, sil),
DEEP WELL(all-c),
RAPID TRANSIT FROM PLACE TO PLACE(all-c)
FEASTING( ant-c, nit-ac, ph-ac, zinc),
SOLEMNITIES( ant-c),
BEING WOUNDED( ant-c)
SOMEONE CALLING OUT(ant-c, merc, sep),
OLD SCHOOLMATE(ant-c, ferr),
OLD FRIENDS( ant-c, ferr),
HOT STOVE(apis),
JUMPING GREAT LEAPS( apis),
BEING A GIRL(apis),
DIRTY ROADS( apis),
WALKING ON DIRTY ROADS(apis),
WALKING OVER HOT FLOOR( apis),
DOGS(arn, sil, sulph, am-c, calc, graph, hyos, lyc, merc, nux-v, op, puls, verat, zinc),
ROMANTIC(am-c),
HORSES(alum, am-c,merc, phos, taent, zinc),
SHAMEFUL(alum, am-c, arn, con, led, staph, tub).
SORE THROAT(bar-c, kreos),
ADVENTUREbar-c, sulph),
WADING IN WATER (ant-t),
PREACHING( ant-t),
PURSUED BY ENEMIES( con),
DEAD FRIEND( arg-n, con, ferr, nat-c),
DEATH OF FRIEND( con, fl-ac, lach),
PURSUED BY SOLDIERS(hyos),
WILD ANIMALS( hyos, lyc, nux-v, sil, sulph, tarent),
BATTLES( all-c, bell, bry, ferr, hyos, sil, thuj),
HISTORIC( cham, mag-c, phos, sil, am-c, ant-t, caust, grph, hyos, merc, sel, stram),
HEARING GUNSHOT(hep),

SHOOTING( merc, hep, spong),

CROCODILE( led),

REMORSE (arn, ars, elaps, fl-ac, lach, led, nat-c, nat-m),

BEING PURSUED BY WILD ANIMALS( sulph, alum, led, nux-v, sil, tarent, verat),

TEETH BREAKING OUT( thuj),

ACCUSATION(lach, nat-m, thuj),

POLLUTION WHICH DID NOT TAKE PLACE( thuja),

DANGER OR DEATH OR ANXIOUS WHEN LYING ON LEFT SIDE( thuja),

WALKING IN MUD( IOD),

WADING IN MUD(IOD),

SOILING HIMSELF(iod),

WALKING IN EXCREMENT( IOD),

DAUGHTER FALLING IN WATER(iod),

MUD(IOD),

SOILING HIMSELF WITH EXCREMENT(aloe, iod, zinc),

UNSUCCESSFUL IN COITION(iod),

DRAGONS(OP),

SKELETON(op),

BEING STABBED,(chin, nat-c, op)

BEING CLOSET(psor),

EXCELLING IN MENTAL WORK( bry, ign, nux-v, sabin, thuj, arn, camph, graph, lach, puls, rhus-t, sabad),

OF HELP( sabad),

DO NOT SUCCEED IN BUSINESS(phos, sabad),

SCIENTIFIC(ign, spong),

DISEASE(nux-v, calc, kreos, lyc),

THEIR ON DISEASE(syp),

BEING PRUD(tub),

JUMPING ( verat),

HUNTING(verat),

BEING STRANGLED(phos, sil, zinc),
BEING SMEARED WITH STOOL(zinc),
DOGS CHANGING INTO HORSES(zinc),
STOOL(aloe, psor, sars, zinc),
monsters( ALOE),
wild (aloe,apis, op),
becoming insane(aloe),
being crazy(aloe),
thunderstorm( arn, ars, nat-c),
making a long speech(arn),
being struck by lightning (Arn),
black dogs( arn,puls),
of death while sleeping on back(arn),
black cats( arn),
violene( arg-n, aur, led,)
darkness ( ars, aur),
people not seen for years( calad),
recalling things long forgotten( sil, am-c, calad, chin, nat-c, sel, sulph),
forest(canth, sep),
stag(canth),
cooking (canth),
walking in woods (canth),
being accused of theft(choc, lach),
journey by car (choc),
gypsies( choc),
guns( choc),
markets(choc),
falling lift (choc),
losing own family( choc),
fortune tellers(choc),
being pregnant( choc),
striving(cina, graph, nux-v, rhus-t, sabin),

drowning of dead bodies(crot-h) ,
smell of dead bodies( calc, crot-h),
churchyard( crot-h),
being in graveyard(crot-h),
falling into pit/abyss ( elaps),
weeping(kreos,sil, elaps, fl-ac, kali-c, mag-, nux-v, spong, stram),
dead friends( arg-n, con, ferr, nat-c),
seeing again an old schoolmate( ant-c, ferr),
dissecting dead bodies( chel, iris, )
seeing autopsies(iris),
dissecting dead bodies(irirs),
he had a fit(iris, sil, mag-c),
suffocation(arn, irirs,kali-bi, kali-c),
beetles(kreos),
glans penis breaking off(kreos),
snow storm(kreos),
dirty linen(kreos),
dirt(kreos),
having taken poison(kreos),
bugs(kroes),
emaciation(kreos),
being pursued by man to violate her(kreos),
lottery(mag-c),
fish(arg-n, kali-c, mag-c),
money(alum, mag-c, phos, puls,zinc),
unsuccessful in finding way to his own house(mag-c),
being soaked in rain ( mag-c),
child bathing in boiling water( mag-c),
unsuccessful in dressing for a event( mag-c),
burnt breast( mag-c),
burnt back( mag-c),
thrown into grave( mag-c) ,

lost at home( mag-c),
obliged to dressing hair in company( mag-c),
cheek burnt( mag-c),
dancing( mag-c),
mask( kali-c, mag-c),
lost in forest( mag-c, sep),
did not wish to make up clothes( mag-c),
difficulties with journey( calc-p, merc, mez, nat-c),
warts( mez),
body part, back, breast, covered with warts (mez),
journey on horse back (nat-c),
ear cut off/cutting (nat-c) ,
being pulled by nose(nat-c),
wedding with two women ( nat-c),
parties((nat-c),
men killed by fallng from high place ( sabin)
sleigh rides (sars)
spiders (sars),
cruelty(nat-m, nux-v, sel, sil)
falling from horse( tarent),
being pursued by bulls(tarent), by animals, wild animals,
horses (alum, am-c, am-m, merc, phos, tarent, zinc)
insults ( tarent)

According to my experience **DREAMS** let you know ***the innermost personality of the person.***

**DREAM** is a specific expression .They reveals a lot. They begins mostly in the evening, a time when threshold of consciousness is lowered & impulses & images of the unconscious can pass across it.

Function of the dream is to restore our ***psychological balance/equilibrium.***

Sometimes what we fail to see/observe during **CASE TAKING** these **DREAMS** pass on the key information to us. After knowing little bit about dream analysis we can cross question our PATIENTS/CLIENTS.

Although we know it is plain ***foolishness to completely believe*** in readymade systematic guides to dream interpretation , as interpretation can vary from person to person according to "Carl jung".

& **HOMOEOPATHY** is all about ***Individualization***.

Finally I will say don't make any ***fixed ideas*** regarding anything. Always keep your focus on ***unbiased***CASE **TAKING** (Never try to skip this).

**Good luck..**

Dr sandeep sairal

9 798887 042794

Printed by Libri Plureos GmbH in Hamburg,
Germany